The Spiri

Rev. Renita Marie Lamkin

P.O. Box 2535
Florissant, Mo 63033

All scriptures are taken from the King James Version of the Bible.

Edited by: Lynel Washington & Brenda Matthews

Cover Artist by Chrissi Nichole Jackson
Book Designer Sheldon Mitchell of Majaluk

Manufactured in the United States of America

Library of Congress Control Number: 2009925347

ISBN 13: 97809816483-9-2
ISBN 10: 0-9816483-9-8

For information regarding discounts for bulk purchases, please contact Prioritybooks Publications at 1-314-741-6789 or rosbeav03@yahoo.com.

You can contact the author at: renitalamkin@yahoo.com.

Published by Prioritybooks Publications
Missouri

Holy Moly!
The Spirituality of Sexuality

Rev. Renita Marie Lamkin

Table of Contents

Reviews   iii

Dedication   v

Acknowledgements   vii

Foreword   ix

Preface   xi

Introduction   xv

Part One
Sexuality and Power   1

I
Redefining First Impressions   4

II
Offensive Encounters   8

III
Adultery   12

IV
Mental Sex   16

V
Remorseful Sex vs. Make-Up Sex   20

VI
Power Sex   *22*

Part Two
Sexuality and Pleasure   **25**

I
Self-Sex   *27*

II
Maintenance Sex   *29*

III
Benevolent Sex   *32*

IV
Menstrual Sex   *34*

V
Anonymous Sex   *36*

Part Three
Sexuality and Passion   **41**

I
Erotic, Adventurous Sex   *44*

II
Alternative Sex   *47*

Part Four
Sexuality and Playful Expression   **49**

I
Flirting   *51*

II
Dating   *53*

Part Five
Sexuality and Prohibitions   *59*

I
Really, It's Not You, It's Me   *61*

II
Body Image   *63*

III
Taboos   *66*

IV
Traumas   *68*

Final Thoughts   *70*

Resources   *71*

Holy Moly!
The Spirituality of Sexuality

Reviews

"I celebrate and applaud Reverend Renita Lamkin's Holy Moly! Through this transparent and revelatory piece the sexual brokenness of women and men will be mended by transformative reflection on the often hidden yet very familiar real-life sexual challenges of many."

Reverend David Aaron Johnson, Pastor
Walker Chapel A.M.E. Church
Seattle, Washington

****

"HOLY MOLY! is right! Finally, a real word from on HIGH that makes it okay to give and receive total and complete love without being damned to hell."

Tammy Tate-Wormly

****

"Holy Moly speaks of the God-given gift of sexuality in a faithful, forthright and affirming way. Reverend Lamkin has given a gift to women who seek to put God first in every area of their life while also enjoying all of God's gifts."

Reverend Robin Roderick, Senior Pastor
First United Methodist Church
St. Charles, Missouri

****

"Holy Moly! is filled with rich wisdom, insight, and **real life stories** for all ages that add a whole new dimension to our marital relationships, our sex life, and our spiritual life with the reality founded that sex is the fundamental fact not only in the operations of nature, but in the construction of God. This book sets women on journeys of healing and can and should be used as a helpful guide toward personal and spiritual wholeness."

Reverend Brenda Jones
Restoring Broken Vessels Ministries
St. Louis, Missouri

****

"Holy Moly! examines, reveals, and then reframes the sensual side of womanhood and married couples as the two become one within the Word of God. Thank you Reverend Renita for reclaiming sex and sensuality as an essential role in the building of relationships after the AMEN!"

Reverend Diana L. Durdin, M.Div.

Dedication

I dedicate this writing to my husband who is

my lover and my friend.

He has taught me to give and receive

love purely—emotionally, spiritually and physically.

Because of his excellence in husbanding, I have

been free to heal and become more whole,

thus making it possible to write from my experiences.

Acknowledgements

To my family and friends who took the time to pre-read and
who provided insightful feedback, thank you.

Rev. Barbara Ballard, LCSW   Rev. Beverly Stith

Rev. Brenda Jones   Rev. Robin Roderick

Rev. Stephen Lamkin   Sandra Gee

Staci Boggeri   Mrs. Elnora Thompson

Mrs. Ernestyne Brown   Gladys Hicks

Allison Richert   Tammy Tate-Wormley

Myron Spencer Davis   Chrissi Jackson

Warlene Reed   Rev. David Johnson

Dr. Pricilla Dowden-White   Imani Williams

Foreword

When I was asked to do a foreward, I approached it with some trepidation. It was my hope that this would be a healing, celebratory, victorious book rather than one of hopelessness, despair and unresolved anger which often emerges in the name of "healing" from sexual issues. How delighted I was to read a refreshing, engaging narrative providing meaningful support for those who have experienced pain in the area of their sexuality.

This is a subject who cries out for our attention and demands our response. Many individuals have miscarried their visions and have allowed the consequences of sexual trauma to affect so many parts of their lives. While many statisticians and religious leaders would deny the high numbers of women, and men, who are living with the scars of sexual trauma, Rev. Lamkin moves it from theory to reality. Many persons in prison have indicated that they are victims of sexual molestation, trauma or abuse. Many women have cried out in private, in women's conferences and with religious leaders only to hear "get over it". Many marriages have failed because of sexual dysfunction resulting from unresolved sexual trauma. The Church is talking more about it but is not providing practical tools for healing, living and renewing sexuality in marriage. This book helps us understand the impact of sexual traumas and taboos and the need for a response.

Rev. Lamkin is to be saluted for her transparency, along with the intellectual presentation of the many perspectives that surround these issues. This is no longer a taboo matter but one that demands a read, with personal and professional engagement. This is the time for such boldness and courage to expose what has been a back room discussion and receive the healing God has provided for our lives.

The Song of Solomon does not shrink in its passionate description of love between a husband and wife. With the level of sexual energy ordained by God, man and woman are more than living souls they are loving souls. How wonderful it is to know that this passion is not just possible but it is attainable and can be a reality.

Relax, this is not a "how to sex" manual for broken people or simply a "how to" manual with your spouse. It is not a step by step approach using some biblical principles; it is a liberating self exploring witness that it is possible to be healed from any hurt, particularly in the area of our sexuality. Depending on your perspective, you may be a little uncomfortable by some of the material. My answer is "great" if it leads to your personal healing or ability to help someone else.

There is hope. There is life. *Dare to believe that you can have more than you ask or think. You are children of the Most High God, and nothing is impossible for you. Conceive it, believe it, and speak it so that you can achieve it. Embrace the fullness of God's power and presence in you and know that God is ready to act and make real what God has planned for you in all parts of your life. This is the day of new beginnings. Live and bring forth life.* *

Holy Moly! This is your day. Read and enjoy.

E. Anne Henning Byfield
The Essence of my Existence 2006

Preface

My husband and I spent Thanksgiving weekend at a retreat cottage in solitude. I read about six books that weekend. Being in solitude with God, my husband, and myself provided an opportunity for my spirit to be cleansed of the toxins and pollutants which had clouded my thoughts, my creativity, and my joy. This time away was the nourishment our souls and relationship needed. I was in school full-time and nearing the end of my degree program. There was a final project coming due, a team project for which I was the editor. Persons on the team were supposed to work on their parts over the weekend. Early in the morning on November 26, 2007, I arrived at my favorite spot—the St. Louis Bread Company®. With my laptop, books, and supplies for a day's work, I felt like I would emerge from my day with the makings of an "A" project. To my irritated surprise there were no e-mails from my teammates. I had an entire day to work on the project, quite possibly the only day I would have, and no project to work on. I e-mailed my classmates and began waiting for their responses.

My soul was fresh and opened so I just started typing. For twelve hours my soul spoke and my fingers typed, completely by-passing my conscious thoughts.

For many years I lived in pain and shame inflicted during my formative years. In childhood I remember that speaking of sex was taboo. Words like "whore" and "slut" were thrown around when it was even thought of that I was with a boy. Standards were set regarding what was and was not proper for women. For example, red fingernail polish and lingerie made a woman a whore. As you read later, I was sexually abused, raped, and martially traumatized. Sex was taught as being *nasty*. Therefore, if you enjoyed sex you were logically nasty. Men were nasty. I learned that there was something about me that made men become nasty.

Given the realities of my past, I would never have pegged myself as writing about sexual experiences, especially as joys. I have discovered that being sexual isn't *nasty*; that being sexual is being natural and vulnerable. I have discovered that being sexual involves coming to terms with your past, being comfortable with your present, and pressing forward for future joys. I have discovered that being sexual involves a spiritual connection with God, yourself, and your spouse.

So, now I write to you my sisters—married, single, and single again. I write to you to tell you about my discovery of self, sexuality, and spirituality as they are interrelated. I write to tell you that you can conquer your past, be it sexual traumas or sexual oppression, you can be free. I write to tell you that married sex can be the best sex of your life and that it is definitely worth the wait. I write to you as a witness that weeping endures for a night—though the night may be long years, —joy does come in the morning! Waking up to enjoy your sexual self is a grand day indeed!

To my brothers reading, I hope that you are able to gain insight into the women in your life. I hope that this writing will help you to develop compassion for the women who have projected their pain onto you, have created unrealistic expectations for you, or have kept themselves locked up from you. I hope this book will help heal your relationships. Loving a woman who has experienced sexual trauma or oppression is no small feat. Gentleness, patience, indulgence, and grace are needed to help her heal. Whether it is your lover's sexual inhibitions or her mood swings that alarm you most, I assure you that through prayer for her, counseling with her, and gentleness toward her, she will heal and emerge into a confident woman.

Please know that I am just a woman, simply writing out of my experiences. This writing is not a clinical voice on sexuality, but rather a personal voice on the issue of spirituality as it relates to our sexuality. I have spent time wrestling with my own ideas. In some cases writing this book has caused me to recognize and wrestle with my perspective on topics—I have been challenged to articulate a liberating view of sexuality and come to terms with my own societal and theological inhibitions. There are topics on which I am yet wrestling. In these areas I offer the subject, the dilemma, the scripture, and the perspective I have formed based upon my careful, prayerful contemplation of the scriptures and writings of psychologists, theologians, and everyday people.

The resources in the back of the book contain information that I have read or surveyed in writing this book. I urge you to seek out a licensed, professional counselor as you are working through your life place.

I do believe there is a lioness inside every woman, waiting and longing for the opportunity to roar. Be brave, my sisters, *Roar*! Your sensual, sexual, spiritual you is waiting to emerge!

Introduction

"Marriage has many pains, but celibacy has no pleasures."

- Samuel Johnson

Marriage is a mystical union between two people. I've been wrestling with and pondering the mystery of marriage for quite some time. How is it that two people can become family who were at one time complete strangers? How can these two people who have met by "chance" become the source of each other's breath?

The answers, at least in part, are found at the intersection of spirituality and sexuality. In this place of meeting, the two become one. The emotional bond that is created is inseparable, except by a force greater than one's faith. When a man fills a woman's physical void with himself, though he withdraws himself physically, he remains with her spiritually. Marital sex is a wonderful blessing from God, a gift from the Great Creator of Life and Love.

Sexuality, especially healthy marital sexuality, is often not spoken of within the Christian community. In church, where many of our values are formed, we most times hear about the consequences of unmarried or extramarital sex, perversions, homosexuality, and fornication. Rarely, if ever, do we hear how God created a means for us to enjoy each other's bodies, to caress each other's spirits. I have never heard a clergy person talk about the beauty and wonderment of the sexual experience.

Sometimes we'll hear how sex was intended for procreation. While I agree that procreation is a result of sex, I don't believe it is the sole reason for sex. If procreation was God's only intention for sex, we'd get pregnant every time we had sex. We probably would not even have sexual longings. We would just mate in season like the animals. When a dog goes into heat she puts off pheromones that attract the male. It is all biology. However, this is not so with humans. The nature of our creation employs us to crave each other. There are times when just thinking about my husband's touch, kiss, and breath sends chills racing through my entire body. This is *not* biology—this is something far more complex. Psychology? In part. Spirituality? Wholly.

In my husband's arms at night I feel safe. I feel secure. I feel like my world is in balance and that everything can be okay. When my husband and I are making love I believe that our spirits are infusing. We aren't just mating, we are relating. I believe sexuality is a way that we honor the God of our being. By enjoying our bodies and connecting our souls we are, in essence, worshiping God with the totality of our beings.

This book begins by looking at the more difficult aspects of sexual experiences and moves toward more pleasant, pleasurable, and passionate experiences. Words have been chosen carefully and intentionally. I share many of my life's details openly for the sake of liberty. It is my intent to neutralize the power of silence that we may all be able to enjoy the beauty and amazement of our sensual, sexual, spiritual selves.

Part One
Sexuality and Power

"If you control someone's sexuality, you control them completely."

Dr. Ted McIlvenna, Methodist Minister

I am certain that sexuality has been perverted and distorted because of the power it possesses. I believe that sex was intended for wonder, amazement, enjoyment, and fulfillment—the mechanism that unifies the two into one. This spiritual unification reminds me of the mysterious indwelling of God's Holy Spirit we experience through our relationship with Jesus. In our flavor of Christianity we understand the Holy Spirit to be the force of power in our Christian life. *"The Spirit helps us with our weakness" and "the Spirit prays for us"* (*Romans 8:26*).

In relationship with our spouses there is a potential for a great infusion of power. The power does not lie in the act of sex itself but rather in the love that inspires sexual encounters. Recently my husband and I had a BIG fight. I was so enraged that I thought I could not stay married to him another minute. I packed an overnight bag and left. I drove around for a few blocks thinking, *Where in the world am I going?* I thought about the great, passionate encounter we had two nights earlier and how I felt as if part of his essence was soaked inside of me. I turned around and came home. I knew what we experienced was real and that I could not stop being connected to him just because I was angry. We worked through our disagreement and continued on with our life. The physical expression of our love translated into an experience that was deeper than emotions—it was spiritual. A spiritual connection is much stronger than emotional connections. Emotions change. When healthy, the spirit of a person doesn't fluctuate; it remains firm in difficult times.

When love is taken out of the sexual equation there is no longer a goal or desire to unify two into one. Instead, the goal or desire is to execute power over another or to prove power over oneself.

Our arch-enemy (Satan, the devil, the deceiver, the evil one) can gain influence in our lives through sexual violence and sexual deceptions. This influence is expressed through hate, guilt, and shame—sometimes toward ourselves and sometimes toward others. I have come to understand that everything God has created, he intended for good (*Genesis 1:10; 50:2)* and the evil forces of the universe twists His good for evil purposes. Because all creative power lies in the heart of God, evil forces must take what God has created and pervert it in order to gain influence in the universe. When our understanding of sexuality is distorted and when our experiences are marred, every aspect of our identity is affected. How we relate to ourselves and how we relate to others, our worth, our value and our values are all affected. God, I believe, intended our sexuality to be a connector of souls. The evil forces of the universe brings division and confusion into our lives through sexual traumas.

I Peter 4:8, *"And above all things have fervent charity among yourselves: for charity shall cover the multitude of sins".* Love covers the sins committed against us by others, sins we commit against others, and sins committed against us by ourselves. We must be able to receive love purely in order to be free. We must heal to love. We must face our hurts to heal.

1
Redefining First Impressions

Our first impression with a person, place or thing generally determines our attitudes, opinions, and understandings. First impressions are not always accurate. I once felt afraid of and inferior to everyone. When people first met me I was accused of thinking I was better than others. There are people who never got to know me because of their first impression of me. What they did not know was that I did not think I was better, I did not feel as if I were adequate. I was afraid. I was afraid of rejection and even more afraid of being accepted for ulterior motives. The first impression people had of me was shaped by my pain. They encountered my wounded spirit and my shame-filled soul.

Similarly, for me, the first encounter with sex shaped my expectations, anxieties, excitements, fears, resentments, ideas, and attitudes about sex. Sex was first introduced to me through encounters with my cousin. I was eight or nine, and he was fifteen or sixteen. Over the next seven years, I would experience sexual traumas through abuse by my neighbor, my youth pastor and neighborhood boys. I was forced to have sex with a neighborhood boy at thirteen, and at fourteen was raped by a different neighborhood boy—well, he was a man in his twenties. At fifteen, I gave birth to a beautiful daughter whose life was entrusted to a wonderful family. Later that year, at the age of sixteen I was forced to have sex by my boyfriend. My spirit was wounded beyond words. A few weeks later I met the man I'd marry at age eighteen. I thought I was in love, perhaps I was for what I knew of love. We had a daughter together when I was seventeen and a son when I was nineteen. After seven years of abuse, often forced sex, and being cheated on, we were finally divorced.

My first impressions with sex planted in me a seed of inhibition. I was always nervous about my body and I could never see my own beauty. I didn't want my first husband to see me naked; I didn't want to see myself naked. I had the idea that married sex should be traditional, in the missionary position, tender, with a lot of kissing and holding and gentleness. With this expectation, my understanding was that anything else was dirty and wrong—*nasty*. When my ex-husband wanted to be spontaneous, fun, or do anything "different", I felt like I was being raped all over again. I couldn't wear red fingernail polish or any lipstick without *feeling* as if I were a "whore". The message about sexuality and about myself as a sexual being were all negative and created a hole in my self-esteem, devalued me as a person, and convinced me that I was a sinful creature unfit for heaven. The spiritual notion of sexual expression was hell, fire and brimstone.

While first impressions are lasting impressions, I am grateful that they do not have to be our final impressions. The initial sexual encounter with my present husband was beautiful. He took his time, exploring every inch of my body, kissing me tenderly, repeatedly asking, "Is this okay?" I still get tingly thinking about it.

What Satan intended for evil, God intended for good in my life. I have been pleasantly surprised at how wonderful our sex life is after eight years of marriage. It's never dull, never hum-drum. Now, I won't go so far as to say that every time feels like the first time, that's romantic non-sense that can most assuredly never be gained.

However, every time is good—real good. Every time satisfies something in my soul and body.

The pain and disgrace of abuse challenges my ability to accept myself as healed and whole. I consistently struggle with my sense of self-worth and value—but praise God I choose to struggle. Caring for my body even today is a decision I have to make daily. I am determined to live life victoriously, free from the effects of abuse. Through prayer, meditation, reflection, counseling, and the compassion of a loving husband, I have had the time and the space to work through the process of healing.

Whatever you have been through, God can heal. I strongly urge you to seek out a licensed, professional, Christian counselor to guide you through the process of healing when you are ready. To heal you must be able to confront the realities of your past and embrace hope for your future possibilities. A woman once told me, "Life is a canceled check you can never get back." You can't change the past, but you can neutralize the pain through the healing process.

I made a decision long ago that I would never allow the enemy to have the final say in my life. I see life as a book. The enemy may begin writing a chapter, but I hold the power of the pen—I get to finish the chapter. I get to determine the way the story ends. I write the conclusion of the matter.

I am only a victim of the circumstances I choose to harbor. Instead of nurturing my pain and licking my wounds I have decided to remove the source of the pain—silence. When we are silent about our suffering, our suffering is intensified by several degrees on the pain scale. When we break the silence, we learn that our experiences are similar to those of others.

I was telling this part of my life story in a women's group one day when a woman said, "Renita, it was not your fault." I wasn't blaming anyone; I was just sharing my story. I wasn't crying about it. I wasn't lashing out in anger. She must have sensed my pain. Those five words unleashed years of pent-up pain and sorrow. It was not my fault. It was not my fault. Now to you, my brothers and sisters I say, it was not your fault. It was not your fault.

Today, most often, the first impression people have of me is generally pleasant. I am real. I am passionate, sometimes impulsive, sometimes wrong, sometimes nonchalant, sometimes overbearing. I am kind and compassionate; irritable and impatient. I am all of these things and they are all really me. By receiving God's healing I have been able to accept being whoever I am at the time and, when necessary, improve what is not cool. Because I have been able to allow God's healing love to saturate my inner being, the wounded spirit and shame-filled soul are no longer the personality that jumps out to greet friends, family, and strangers. I have redefined that first impression.

The same is true with our sexual experiences. When we are healed, we are able to redefine our first impressions. By approaching sexuality through our healed spirituality, we are able to see the sexual beauty within ourselves and experience the sexual beauty of our spouse as our lovers.

II
Offensive Encounters

Nothing is as sure to block the freedom of the spirit like being offended. Offended, in this section, refers to sin. We are many times guilty of sinning—offending someone else. Likewise, we are also often offended—others sin against us.

When I was a child there were no warnings against pedophiles. There were no teachings about "stranger danger." We were not cautioned about those who would abuse us. We were not allowed to speak badly about adults. We had no opinion that really mattered and were rarely, if ever, heard. Because of the cultural climate of that era (some twenty years ago) children were abused and suffered in silence. The real tragedy is that the silence has followed us into adulthood. In many cases instead of talking about our struggles we just act out. Certainly, I will not assert that the single cause of pain is sexual offenses. However, I do believe that offenses against our sexuality are a leading cause of the pain women suffer.

Being told that we are ugly, too dark, too light, too tall, or too short, too fat or too thin are offenses against our sexuality. We compare our breasts to those of other women and our hair, cheek bones, thighs, calves, abdominal area, and buttocks are all areas open for attack. These attacks wound our spirit and create a sense of disconnect between the way we feel and the way we think we *should* feel.

For the sake of liberation, in this section I will briefly discuss some areas of sexual offenses. Certainly these are not the only areas of offense. Perhaps they are just the most common, or at the very least, the most common to me.

I believe that some reading this book will be able to identify with the areas of offenses and may, for the first time, be able to admit having been offended. Perhaps you were offended in some other way. Whatever the offense, once we are able to admit having been offended, we will be able to release the offender and cleanse our spirit of the offense. Victims become victors when we break free of the offender's power.

Offensive encounters are those which exploit the authority, strength, relationship, or power a person has in relationship to the victim. Some such scenarios are those in which the victim has a disadvantage due to age, reduced mental or physical capacity, or lack of will.

Children and adolescents are the most vulnerable groups to sexual offenders. I feel the unction to say that there are never circumstances that make it okay for an adult to engage in any type of sexual activity with a child or adolescent. There was a girl in high school bragging about having had sex with a very handsome teacher. From what I now know, I must wonder if she were bragging or crying out. Men are not the only sexual perpetrators. Statistically, boys don't report being molested or raped by women. Having sex with an older woman is most often seen as a rite of passage or a conquest. If you were offended as a child it was not your fault—not even if you were an adolescent with an adult's body.

Date rape is another area of offense never spoken of when I was younger. There was the understanding that if a girl didn't want anything to happen then she shouldn't put herself in the situation where there is an opportunity; that she shouldn't wear clothes which would provoke a man's desires; and that she shouldn't lead a man on. For these reasons I lived with the shame of having had sex. That shame caused me to feel unworthy of being loved and appreciated. Feeling unworthy leads to self-abuse as well as attracts more abuse. It is a vicious circle that can have an end.

If there was ever a time in your life that you said no and his yes overpowered your no, you were offended against. No means no. It is time to shake that thing off. As women we must be free from these offenses!! Spending our lives trying to control our lives will not take away the fear, disgust, resentment, and pain we experienced when our "no" was ignored. Set your spirit free!!

It is never acceptable for persons to take sexual advantage of our elders. Senior sexual abuse is on the rise. A sexual offense occurs if there is not the mental ability to make sound judgments, the physical ability to refuse advances, or the emotional ability to say no. This is a definition of rape.

It is offensive for a person to bring animals into the sexual relationship. This is bestiality. I read an article in a women's magazine once about a woman whose husband had an animal fetish. He wanted her to participate in his animal encounters. She talked about how dirty she felt, knowing that these acts were wrong, but felt as if she had no one to talk to. It was unfortunate that she gave way to his offenses until he died. In marriage we vow to love, honor, and cherish our spouses. If our sexual urges cause harm to our spouse, we must deny ourselves the right to be satisfied. Loving requires sacrifice. Satisfying a sexual urge over demonstrating love to the spouse creates an offense.

Being offended sexually wounds the spirit. Know, my sisters and brothers, that it was the offender who hurt you, not the sexual act. It is important to separate the two, even though doing so is extremely difficult. When you are able to sever the action from the offender you will be able to more fully enjoy sexual acts with a spouse-lover. It is difficult to move forward in living with offenses clogging the arteries of the spirit. Sometimes we've just got to say it out loud, "I was raped." "I was abused." "I was molested." "<u>This person</u> did <u>*this act*</u> to me." Saying this out loud doesn't make the offense more real and it doesn't make the offense happen again. Saying it out loud breaks the silence of the secret shame. Breaking the silence frees the pain!

When Jesus commanded Lazarus to rise from the tomb, he commanded that the grave clothes be loosed. As you read this today, my sisters, Jesus is calling you out of your tombs of pain and desires that you be freed from your grave clothes. In the name of Jesus I pray - the grave clothes—shame, guilt, pride, control, disappointment, anger, resentment—be loosed from your spirit! Accept liberty and healing! Be loved! Be free!

III
Adultery

The most immediate thought of the adulterer is of a man sneaking around with some woman. Well, women commit adultery too. I committed adultery in my first marriage. The relationship with my ex-husband was deflated. He was violent and abusive, irresponsible and irrational. I was in a pit of hopelessness and thought that I could never have a life better than the one I lived. I met a man (well, we were both only twenty-something) who made my spirit come alive. He talked to me and showed me value. As they say, "one thing led to another" and that was that. It was hard breaking off the relationship because he really cared about me. I was so full of guilt and disdain for myself that I committed even more to remaining in my destructive marriage. Having sex with a man who was not my husband had nothing at all to do with the sex, but had everything to do with the hole in my soul.

Adultery is a violation of the covenant made before God and can never be justified, regardless of the terrible nature of the marriage relationship. Proverbs 6:32 says *"But whoso committeth adultery with a woman lacketh understanding: he that doeth it destroyeth his own soul."* Perhaps the understanding one lacks is of the spiritual connection of the sexual act. Perhaps the destruction of the soul is due to the severing of the spiritual connection between the adulterer and spouse and the adulterer and God.

I wonder if there are natural laws against adultery because women were the property of the men they married. Under Napoleonic code adultery was only a crime for women. Adultery is still a crime in many states in America. Punishment ranges from death to a ten dollar fine.

Although I am uncertain of the motives of the natural laws, I am persuaded that adultery is spoken of in the scriptures because of the spirituality of sexuality. If our spirit infuses with another, as I previously asserted, the spiritual connection between husband and wife are severed when we have sex with another.

If you have ever been cheated on you can probably relate to this. A husband or wife just "knows" when the spouse has been unfaithful even when there is absolutely no physical evidence. I am convinced by my own experiences that we *know* because we *feel* the bond is severed. When my ex-husband had a "girlfriend" while we were married (he had several throughout our marriage) I *knew* it long before there was evidence. There was something different about the way he behaved. There was something different about the way he interacted with me. There was something different about the way I felt in his presence. There was something different.

When a woman has been powerless, for whatever reason—poverty, abuse, low self-esteem—sex can become a weapon we can use against other women, against our husbands, and essentially against ourselves.

Against other women: Sex gives a woman power, the "upper hand". I have observed women who will flaunt themselves, their boobs, butts, and brains over a man. I have listened to women talk about their ability to get someone else's man. When women resort to using their sexual power to be powerful, another woman usually ends up hurt. I have known of families destroyed because of a woman's need to be "more than" another woman. I believe what these women fail to realize is that they are not demonstrating their power they are displaying their weakness, their own lack of identity, self worth, and confidence.

Against our husbands: I had a friend whose husband had several affairs. Fed up with his infidelity she decided to get back at him by having an affair of her own. She did not count on the consequences. Her husband was able to prove her affair although she was unable to prove his. He filed for divorce and she had to pay him alimony. He got the kids. She developed feelings for her "fling" and spent a long time confused and depressed.

Against ourselves: Sex sometimes is the only way a woman knows how to fight back against the pain of her life. Women are notorious for filling their emptiness with sex and for using sex as a way to mask the pain of their past and present. I know a woman who had many adulterous affairs. There was nothing seriously wrong in her marriage. She appeared to have a great life. She was hurting from her life. Just as some turn to alcohol, she had sex.

Sometimes women consciously or unconsciously believe that if a man wants to have sex with her she should do it. It doesn't register that it is wrong until it's too late to turn back. There's a type of emotional conditioning that sets in when a woman has experienced sexual traumas. This conditioning is to comply or be a failure. Comply or be in trouble. Comply or be ridiculed. Comply or be hurt— physically, emotionally, and/or spiritually.

There are no loopholes in marriage. If our spouse doesn't arouse us or doesn't take interest in us or doesn't love us or provide for us (or whatever) we don't get to violate our covenant. Marriage is a vow that is made before God. When the vow is violated, our relationship with God is broken.

We do not have the right to use sex as a weapon or as a pacifier. We have to deal with our lives, past and present. We have to face our realities and work through our difficulties. Repairing our spirit is the beginning to healing our sexual behaviors, attitudes, and values.

If you are now or have in the past been involved in adultery, please seek emotional and spiritual guidance. Just stopping the affair will not heal the areas of brokenness that enticed you into the affair(s) to begin with. While you may be able to cut out the sex, if the pain is still there, you'll fill your void by abusing something else—food, substance abuse, shopping, excessive church work. Seek counseling from your pastor and/or a licensed, trained therapist.

There is GREAT NEWS for the adulterer/ adulteress: Jesus forgives. Jesus heals. Jesus redeems. Jesus repairs. Jesus restores. Through the power of the great love of God we can be restored!

Adultery does not have to end a marriage, but it will take a lot of work to repair the relational damage an affair causes. Commit yourself to the work and it will be a worthwhile journey!

IV
Mental Sex

"Whatsoever things are pure, just, lovely, and of good report think on these things." Philippians 4:8.

Sexual encounters are not always acted out physically. The imagination station can be an exciting, stimulating, and dangerous place for your sexual encounters to occur. Mental sex can lead one to committing sexual offenses. A person who is stimulated by false images (picture, voices) will always find themselves disappointed, lacking, and wanting more. A problem is that our lusts and desires can never be quenched. They are like a rapidly burning fire, consuming all other desires in their path. One pornographic picture or movie can be the spark that sets the mind ablaze. When that "more" cannot be found with the spouse, one often turns to another for gratification.

As children we sang, "Oh be careful little eyes what you see. For the Father up above is looking down in love." What we see with our eyes and hear with our ears enters into our minds and seeps into our hearts. It goes from being an "interest" or a "past time" or "entertainment" to a desire, longing, and need.

In the scriptures we are taught to take into captivity every imagination that presents itself against the knowledge of God. 2 Corinthians 10:5 says, "Casting down imaginations, and every high thing that exalteth itself against the knowledge of God, and bringing into captivity every thought to the obedience of Christ." God's knowledge regarding sexuality teaches that sexuality is not merely physical, it's relational and spiritual— "And Adam knew Eve..." (Genesis 4:1). Relational sexuality is between two people in a relationship, not a person and an image.

It is unfair to hold a spouse to the image created in media. It is unfair to expect a spouse to perform as the actors/actresses in porno flicks. When our sexual desires are so numb that it takes artificial stimulation to awaken them, it is time for us to begin seeking God, the giver of desires for an awakening from within. Proverbs 5:15 says, "Drink water from thine own cistern…" If the waters at home are bitter, seek God for a sweetening. Pray that until the waters sweeten you will acquire a taste for the water that's yours.

When illness or impotence prevents one from enjoying sexual activities, the physical desires can become an obsession in the mind. My husband was ill for many months. During his illness there was little sexual contact. I prayed that God would take my sexual desires away; however, it seemed like the less he wanted sex, the more I craved it.

I saw a man in a restaurant; he was very good looking and we made eye contact. He kept talking to me with his face, waiting on an invitation to speak. When he got up and walked my way, I looked aside, deliberately refusing myself the opportunity for conversation. I was vulnerable. My sexual senses were heightened. I was probably sending out some sex signal that attracted men.

I realized that day that I was having sex in my mind which violated my marital covenant. My mental sex was not with the gorgeous man, but with my husband. In my mind, the desire for sexual gratification was overpowering my commitment to "love, honor, and cherish in sickness and in health." I wasn't cherishing my husband, and my resentment was not honoring him.

After repenting, I fasted from all needless pleasures—for me this was sodas, sweets, and meats. I got a pedicure and joined the fitness center near our home. I worked out my sexual energy, and in the sauna I sweated out my sexual frustrations. Through the disciplining of my physical appetite I was able to gain control over my sexual appetite. Regaining focus on my spiritual self took focus off my physical self. When I cleared my mind from physical expectations my body stopped yearning for what it could not have.

The point here is this: "Thou wilt keep him in perfect peace, whose mind is stayed on thee: because he trusteth in thee" (Isaiah 26:3). We will give attention to whatever is most on our mind. Keeping our minds on God is more than just thinking about "heavenly" things. Keeping our minds on God includes focusing on that which will lead to peace and ultimately to one's contentment. There are times when we have to intentionally focus on the good in our relationships, even if there are only drops and dribbles. I can hear the screams of women (and men) who resent the notion of contentment. The reality of mature relationships is that contentment is sometimes a blessing. The Apostle Paul said, "Not that I speak in respect of want: for I have learned, in whatsoever state I am, therewith to be content." (Philippians 4:11). The spirituality of sexuality extends far beyond what our minds and bodies believe to be "great sex." The spirituality of sexuality provides for our mental and spiritual peace (well-being) during difficult physical times. When the relationship is healthy we can look at others of the opposite sex and not have a desire for that person. When the relationship is healthy we can merely think about our spouses and experience a grand awakening!

Mental sex can be exciting and non-offensive when the sexual partner is our spouse and the sex is expectation of what is to come as opposed to longing for what one cannot have.

V
Remorseful Sex vs. Make-Up Sex

Using sex to "fix" a marital problem is "remorseful sex" and it can be offensive to the hurting spouse. In remorseful sex, one or both partners initiate sex to cover the relational pain and avoid dealing with the depth of the issues. In this manner, remorseful sex is the same as drinking, drugging, eating, shopping, gambling, etc. to cover life's pain. When sex is used as a mask, it becomes a way to deceive rather than a way to heal. When a relationship is in trouble there are always violations of respect, honor, and dignity. Sex, even great sex, does not cure the hurts of our heart. Having sex, even great sex, doesn't mean that the relationship is okay. A couple must be willing to engage in the process of restoration and reconciliation. Since this can be a painful process, it is sometimes easier to just comb over the issues with sex and pretend like everything is okay afterward.

Sex can only say "I'm sorry" when the other person's gift of sex is saying "I forgive you." "I'm sorry" and "I forgive you" must happen at the same time in order for sex to be healing to the spirit. When the giver and receiver of forgiveness are in a mutual spiritual place, the healing power of the couple's love can propel them into sexual expression of their spiritual reconciliation.

I cannot show my husband how sorry I am for hurting him by how passionately I make love with him. I show him how sorry I am by admitting my faults and making a conscious effort to modify my hurtful behaviors. Sex then becomes a way to seal the promises to love, honor, and cherish. This is often termed "make-up sex."

I feel compelled to tell you that once you have sealed your promises to love, honor, and cherish and have agreed to forgive each other you cannot bring up the forgiven offenses in the future without unsealing the wound. *"Love covers a multitude of sins" (1 Peter 4:8).* Through sexual intercourse, there is a type of love covering that occurs—this is part of the spirituality of sexuality, a mystical occurrence shared by those whose sexual relationship transcends physical boundaries. When sins have been covered to uncover is to essentially renounce the spiritual aspect of your sexual encounter. This may be the greatest of all sexual offenses.

Experiencing the transforming power of love requires discipline. Pray that the Holy Spirit will help you discipline your emotions and empower the pureness of your love expressions. Through the great gift of reconciliation, there is a promise for relational restoration.

VI
Power Sex

In many relationships sex becomes a leveraging or bargaining tool. Sometimes sex is used as a reward for "good" behavior or withheld as a consequence for "bad" behavior. There are so many shades of grey in this area of sexuality. We naturally feel more inclined to have sex with our spouses when we are feeling good about the relationship. When our spouse is doing all the things we think he or she ought to do we feel valued and honored. When we experience this level of respect we more naturally feel good about the relationship. Feeling good makes us more inclined to desire each other physically.

However, when all of the pieces aren't together, one or both partners can feel neglected and wounded. Maintaining our responsibilities in role assignments creates balance. Parenting, cleaning house, paying bills, cooking dinner, washing clothes, yard care, marriage-friendship building, home repairs, car repairs, civic participation, and church participation are some of the tasks each spouse takes ownership of in a marriage. Whatever the agreements are, the relationship is in balance when each partner does what he or she agreed to do. *Agreed to* is an important factor here. If the roles are assumed roles or dictated roles, bitterness and resentment are inevitable. It is my experience that role balance and responsibility in the family and/or relationship nurtures the spirit of the relationship.

When tasks are left undone, the partners usually begin feeling as if the commitment to the relationship has been breached. It is normal for a partner to feel unvalued, disrespected, taken for granted, and imposed upon when tasks are left undone. This breach wounds the spirit. Naturally a person does not want to have sex when the spirit has been wounded. Without clear communication it can feel as though a partner is being punished for not doing the dishes or cutting the grass. Communication can make it clear that the spouse is feeling hurt.

When the bills are paid, dinner is cooked, laundry is finished, sheets are clean, and the car is running it is natural to feel valued, treasured, appreciated, and respected. Fulfilling one's role in the relationship nurtures the spirit, creating an environment where sexual desires are also nurtured.

Power sex is when one partner uses sex to manipulate the other into doing something or withholds sex punitively for what a partner hasn't done, or as a consequence for something the partner *did* do and shouldn't have. The difference between power sex and the sexual expression of a nurtured spirit is in the motive. The motive of power sex is manipulation. Power sex is using sex to get what you want. If a couple desires spirituality in their sexuality, sex cannot be used to get your way or to punish. There's simply not much difference between "If you do this, I'll do that" and "If you pay me $100 I'll do this." Marital prostitution is not a spiritual expression of sexuality.

I Corinthians 7:5 says, "Defraud ye not one the other, except it be with consent for a time, that ye may give yourselves to fasting and prayer; and come together again, that Satan tempt you not for your incontinency." Prayer and fasting are the only reasons to abstain willfully from sexual sharing. And note even then, abstaining is by agreement.

The instructions to "stop depriving" are words of wisdom, not law. We are not *obligated* to have sex because we are married; however, deprivation leads to temptation. This is not out of spite necessarily, but rather, out of human flesh. A wife's attempt to "teach him a thing or two" may result in her learning something she didn't want to know.

Husbands, if your wives are withholding maliciously, you cannot "show her" that "a man has needs" by violating the marital covenant. She is hurting, regardless of how angry and mean she is behaving. Pray for your wife's healing. Pray for God to show you why she is hurting so badly. And women, if it is your husband, the same applies.

It is extremely important to marital health and longevity to "not let the sun go down on your anger." When the spirit has been wounded and sexual desire has fizzled, the couple must have an honest conversation. Fixing what's broken is hard enough; not knowing what's broken makes the fixing impossible. When your spouse's behavior affects your spirit, you must be willing to share your sense of pain as opposed to a sense of entitlement. Husbands and wives owe only one thing to one another, and that is to love (*Romans 13:8*). We don't owe each other our bodies. We simply owe love in our relationship.

Part Two
Sexuality and Pleasure

Pleasure is a necessary reciprocal. No one feels, who does not at the same time give it. To be pleased, one must please. What pleases you in others, will in general please them in you.

Lord Chesterfield

Certainly there are good, healthy aspects to sexuality. Up to this point I've discussed the heavier side of sexuality. It is my experience that sex cannot be fun nor fully appreciated until we have been healed of sexual offenses.

There are many restrictions placed upon the sexual expression of our love. Admittedly, I am not as in tune to what young people are being taught today. However, when I was a teen we were taught that fulfilling "sinful pleasures" brought perversion into the marriage. Women ought to be "chaste" and "discreet."

I have grown to believe that there can be an "anything goes" rule in the marital relationship. Of course, there's always an escape clause! Anything goes can only be in effect when both partners agree. If both partners are not in agreement what was intended for pleasure turns into an offense. In the following pages we'll explore some of these areas of sexuality and the infusion of spirituality.

I
Self-Sex

I have heard a good deal of Christian teaching against masturbation. However, I have not found the scripture to back up the teaching. I have heard conservative teachings from preachers, teachers, and caring women who say that sex with yourself—masturbation, fondling, caressing—is fornication. One preacher I heard said that if you're married, masturbation is adultery.

Masturbation is most often thought of as a man's issue, or privilege depending upon your perspective. I remember hearing the threat of a man going blind if he masturbated. I cannot recall having ever been taught one way or another in regards to women and masturbation. I figured, however, if one thought of masturbation as a sin for men it would surely be also considered so for women.

Now, I want to spend a minute talking about the issue of fornication. This term is quite often used in Christian teachings and can be misrepresented. Fornication is human sexual intercourse—sexual contact between two people with at least one person's genitalia. A person cannot fornicate with themselves. In this case, it really does take two to tango!

With this understanding I do not believe masturbation fits the definition of a sexual sin. I know that this statement will be very shocking to those who have been taught and have taught differently, just breathe, it's okay, really.

Another perspective I have heard is that masturbation is merely releasing sexual/hormonal pressure, purely physical in nature. There are some who contend that relieving yourself sexually is as natural and harmless as urinating.

Masturbation is really a great way for a woman to explore her own body and please herself. It is not always possible, or reasonable for us to expect, that our husbands will hit the "right" spot to please us. When we know for ourselves where our "spot" is, we'll be able to guide our husbands. Sometimes, he'll get finished before we do. It's okay to continue getting your groove on, even if you gotta groove all by yourself!

Women are conditioned to be caretakers and nurturers. This conditioning, for many women, is carried over into our sex lives and we often forego our own gratification in order to please our man. Sisters, it is okay to *expect* to be sexually satisfied. Sometimes you've just got to help a brother out!

I must say; however, if a person is masturbating in front of pictures, movies, computer images, phone voices, or mental images, I do not believe it to be an example of having self-sex (a purely physical act or a mere release of sexual pressure). I believe that this is sex with whoever is on the other end of the vocal, visual, or cyber image. This is, in my opinion, adultery in the heart.

My advice is this: If you start to touch yourself and you feel convicted then stop. If it is sin *to* you, it is sin *for* you. Seek God's answer for your life. If your convictions do not lead you toward masturbation being a sin, this outlet can bring you or your spouse relief when you are separated by miles, menstruation, or sleep.

II
Maintenance Sex

Maintenance sex happens when we've worked long hours, spent little time together, and are dead tired and both partners feel at least somewhat aroused. When our bodies are tuned in to each other we may want to have sex even when our brain and energy are shutting down. Routinely denying or depriving ourselves or each other of sexual stimulation is not healthy for the marriage. There are chemical triggers in our brain that need to be released. Research actually reveals that women who have a healthy sex life also have a generally more pleasant disposition. Maintenance sex helps us to feel connected to our spouse in spite of long days and busy evenings.

If you haven't heard the term "maintenance sex" before, perhaps you are more familiar with "quickie." A quickie is the type of sex you have when you either lack the time or the energy to really do your thang. If you wait for the right time or for when you have enough time; if you wait until you are "in the mood" and full of energy weeks if not months can pass by without an encounter. This is not healthy for your marriage or for your chemistry.

Maintenance sex holds a great deal of value in the marital relationship. A sexual relationship without routine maintenance (spiritual, emotional and physical) will be less enjoyable and may eventually fall apart. I do not believe it is reasonable for most couples who are married, working, and dealing with the complexities of life to have passionate, erotic sex as a routine. Maintenance sex will hold the couple over until desire, time, energy, and privacy allow for more exciting encounters.

When sexual encounters become more maintenance, and passionate encounters are fewer and farther between, it's time to examine the relationship. For women, perhaps more so than with men, when our emotions are out of whack it is difficult to become aroused physically. Somehow we are created in such a way that our emotional self and our physical self are wired together. When we are off balance spiritually and emotionally, having sex is very difficult, being passionate is nearly impossible, and being erotic is out of the question!

Examine the environment. Stress reduces the sex drive. A cluttered house, a cluttered bedroom, lack of routine, excessive noise, funny smells (which could include scented candles and incense), too much/too little light can be environmental stress triggers.

Examine your routine. Are you having maintenance sex because you are *always* tired? Why are you so tired? Why are you so busy? Is what you're doing more important than the marital covenant? Here's something to ask yourself: Do you busy yourself to avoid sexual encounters with your spouse? Be honest now. If so, you must, for the health of your soul, your relationship, and your family explore why this is so. Perhaps sexual avoidance is due to an unhealed wound in the past. Perhaps sexual avoidance is due to a conflict with your spouse.

I most often hear of women who are too tired for sex. The most common complaint I hear is how busy women are and emotionally drained from all of the work and emotional caretaking they do throughout the day. As a wife I know that our husbands can also be too tired, emotionally drained, and too stressed to have sex. I invite you to look at the load of life your spouse is carrying. There are almost always ways to pitch in and carry part of the load for the one you love. *"Bear ye one another's burdens, and so fulfill the law of Christ" (Galatians 6:2).*

CAUTION

If you are only pitching in with domestic chores, or paying bills, or such in order to access the sexual portal, you are treading in dangerous waters. Remember: Healthy, marital sexuality begins with a spiritual connection. Mature love is understood to include a willingness to sacrifice time, energy, schedule, ideas, and desires in order to bless each other "Greater love hath no man than this,that a man lay down his life for his friends." (John 15:13). Laying down our personal agenda to help ease the burden of our spouse is a way to show love to our spouses. Please note, if the sense of helping is to get something, burdens have just been traded rather than relieved (i.e., dishes for sex). When sex becomes a chore the whole relationship is affected.

Maintenance sex should just hold you over until you can relax and enjoy the exhilaration of passion and the adventure of the erotic. If all you are having is maintenance sex you are missing out on a wonderful aspect of married sex. I believe however, that maintenance sex is better than not having sex at all. So if maintaining is the best you or your spouse can offer each other—maintain!

III
Benevolent Sex

Benevolence is love and charity, not force and control. The longer you are in a relationship the more opportunities you will have to share with your spouse what I call benevolent sex.

It is common that both partners will not always feel like having sex at the same time. Out of love for the other we sometimes give ourselves even when we don't feel like it. This is a gift we give to each other and a reflection of the spirituality of our relationship. We don't always have to "feel" like pleasing the other. Mature lovers please each other for the other one's pleasure. Mature love is not self-centered or self-focused.

An important aspect of this area of married sex is remembering that the scripture teaches us to not withhold ourselves from each other (*I Corinthians 7:3-5*). I understand these to be words of wisdom, not law. Having said that, I have learned through my experience, if his physical love is rejected his emotional love will diminish, over time. You may not like that truth, but it is truth, nonetheless. Sexual pleasure is like a comfort for all of the emotional, physical, and financial hardships family life demands.

If you are choosing to share the gift of benevolence with your spouse you must make it believable. Now, some will say that this is "faking it." I disagree. While one may have to consciously think about making the sounds and motions more so associated with passionate sex, it is still *real*. It is a real expression of love and a real expression of pleasure. If you are just laying there making your spouse do all the work and essentially only participating by providing your body you are not having sex of any kind—your spouse is. This could make a spouse feel rejected and diminished.

It's okay to give your spouse the gift of yourself even when you're not feelin' it. I may not always be feelin' *it;* but because I am feelin' *him,* he'll be *feelin'* me!

IV
Menstrual Sex

Christian teaching varies on whether a couple should have sex during the menstrual cycle. Leviticus 15 talks about abstaining from sex while a woman is having her "flow." Leviticus also says that a woman should not go into the temple until she has been "clean" for seven days. Leviticus also talks about sprinkling the blood of pigeons and burning incense as an act of repentance.

A dilemma this subject presents is in knowing what part of the law a person should adhere to and what part should one release. For me, if I were to abstain from having sex during my period for scriptural purposes I would also, then, refrain from going to church while menstruating. To me, that doesn't seem reasonable. I don't follow the law regarding pork. I eat some meat that is not well-done. I don't keep all of the law. Or do I? Jesus said that the summary of the law is this, *"Thou shalt love the Lord your God with all thy heart, all thy soul and with all thy mind. This is the first and great commandment and the second is like unto it, Thou shalt love your neighbor as thyself. On these two commandments hang all the laws and the prophets" (Matthew 22:34-40).* I believe that we are under the law of grace as opposed to the rules of the Mosaic laws.

In the structure of the Ten Commandments, loving God is wrapped up in the first five, loving my neighbor is in the second five. Honoring the commandments is not following a legalist set of rules—it is honoring the meaning, or the spirit, of the rules—loving God and loving my neighbor as myself.

My theological understanding allows me the freedom to engage in intercourse during my period. My preference; however, is to not have intercourse during my menstrual time and my husband honors my preferences.

Please note that menstrual sex does not have to be penetrating sex. During our cycle we can still enjoy the sensual pleasures of sexuality and provide sensual pleasures to our husbands. Spooning, oral sex, and hand sex are avenues one can explore during this time.

This is *my* view. It is important for you to honor the beliefs of your convictions. If it feels like sin *to* you, it is sin *for* you and you must abstain. If it doesn't bother you physically or spiritually, enjoy! Some women report having easier cycles, less cramping, and less blood flow when they have sex while on their cycle.

Remember, sex in marriage is for procreation and the building and maintaining of a healthy, exciting relationship. My desire for women is that each of us would have the internal and relational freedom to express ourselves sexually in ways that are physically satisfying, emotionally nurturing and spiritually healthy.

V
Anonymous Sex

Can one have sex just to satisfy the physical need without any spiritual-emotional consequence? Anonymous sex in this section refers to sex where there is seemingly no emotional or spiritual connection—one strives to maintain emotional-spiritual anonymity during the course of the sexual relationship.

A person cannot have sex without an emotional and spiritual consequence; every action has a corresponding reaction. Sometimes the reaction sparked may be positive and sometimes the reaction may be negative; but never do our actions produce neutral results.

Sometimes we can numb ourselves to the negative consequences and tell ourselves that "it's nothing," when really it is something. We can numb ourselves for so long in our desire to satisfy our pleasures that when we want to have an emotional, spiritual experience, we struggle to connect.

After the divorce from my first husband, I discovered the exhilarating pleasure of having sex. Yes, I was a single woman having unmarried sex. Not only was I having unmarried sex, I was in church every Sunday and really loving the Lord. Although I was convicted before I'd get to grooving and remorseful after, the pleasure overwhelmed my moral and spiritual beliefs and values.

Part of the pleasure was in discovering that I could be in control and that I had power over the man. It wasn't just my physical need that was being met; it was my need for power and control that was being met. Having lived a life of being a victim, I finally had the opportunity to exert control over a man and over myself. Sex was almost like a drug, the more we did it the more I wanted to do it, the more I *had* to do it. I *had* to do it because the physical pleasure overwhelmed the spiritual and emotional pain. I was in a vicious, destructive cycle.

Fortunately this spell didn't last very long. I was blessed to discover within a matter of six months that my need for power and control was rooted in the life pain I was still bearing; that wielding power did not heal the pain. I was blessed to discover that the physical pleasure I shared with a man was not worth the emptiness and loneliness that anonymous sex left behind. I am grateful that I learned quickly. I was able to heal from my self-inflicted pain and preserve myself for the husband God promised.

We just cannot refrain from having sex that is emotionally and spiritually anonymous. The connection may not be felt right away, but every action has a corresponding reaction—a consequence we must deal with eventually.

Having sex for pleasure is different from experiencing sexual pleasure. I believe that the New Testament teachings regarding abstaining from premarital sex has more to do with protecting us than regulating us. Jesus' ministry is marked by his willingness to go against the norms, shake up the status quo, challenging traditional thought, liberating the oppressed, and empowering the weak. With that ministry in mind, I cannot believe that God created us as sexual beings in order to trap us in sin. Our sexual desires are designed to bless our lives. The sexual relationship, I believe, was designed for the infusing of two into one, creating a soul tie unintended for severing.

Each time we give our bodies to someone we are creating a tie. When the relationship is healthy the couple grows together—becomes one. When the relationship is toxic, the toxicity pollutes your spiritual system and eventually seeps into every aspect of your life.

This concept may be hard for someone to believe if they do not have emotional feelings for a person. The tie is not caused by feelings, it's caused by the act of sex itself. So, each time you change partners you sever the tie with the previous. This process of severing is not as clean cut as putting your head on a chopping block although it's just as messy. This process of severing is more like cutting with a dull knife, pieces are left jagged, raggedy, and hanging on.

With jagged, raggedy edges and sexual sins hanging on, we are less able to present ourselves unto God as living sacrifices, holy and acceptable unto Him. When we are all jacked up we cannot bless the people around us, including our children, our close family members, and our friends. We cannot discover the greatness that lies within us when we are jagged and raggedy in our spirit. Because we are created for God's glory we have the responsibility to live a life that glorifies God. It's not called a living sacrifice for nothing. We must present our best, unblemished self to God.

For those who have become good at blocking emotional ties the consequences may not be evident until one is in a loving, marital relationship and unable to emotionally connect with their spouse.

I caution you, children of the Most High, guard your spirit. Your spirit is as fragile as it is powerful. Be careful who you let into your spirit. Your body may want him, but he may be poison to your spirit—every action has a corresponding reaction. It may be all good now and a hot mess later. Use your power for good—exercise your power over your own desires. Embrace your fragility with honor—you are God's handiwork.

I experienced healing through the grace of God. When the emotional and spiritual reality of my behavior was revealed, I immediately confessed my sin to God and received God's forgiveness and changed my behavior. Perhaps you are in a vicious circle of what you believe to be anonymous sex. Please seek help from God, a professional therapist, and/or a qualified spiritual leader. If you go to church, keep going. The power of God's word will break through the power of Satan's stronghold and you will be free.

Part Three
Sexuality and Passion

"It does not matter what you do in the bedroom as long as you do not do it in the street and frighten the horses."

Mrs. Patrick Campbell

For me, passion begins long before the bedroom door closes. Passion begins when I wake up in the morning, sharing conversation with my husband before we dart out the door. Passion builds throughout the day when we share sweet, encouraging messages. Passion simmers in the evening exchange of the day's activities, when we're sharing family time, or enjoying evening television together. After the final good nights are said, the bedroom door is closed, and the lights are turned down. When we snuggle together, with him holding me close, passion intensifies as he prays for our family, our church, our friends, even our dog. He prays for me—my dreams and desires, encouragement for my disappointments, and direction for my path. I pray for him—for the load he carries as husband, father, pastor, son, brother, advisor, and friend. We say our "amens" and snuggle close together, our passion burns hotter.

Passion is having yourself under control, blending intensity with gentleness. Passion is *feeling* each other's body and breath. Passion is taking your time, each move leading into the next. Passion smells the essence of each other, tastes the sweetness of each other's lips, the saltiness of each other's skin, feels the taste buds on each other's tongue. Passion does not hurry. Passion lingers and reflects while the heart of the passionate beats loudly and with strength.

Passion is more than bodies touching. Passion is souls merging. Passion is feeling like there is no closeness that is close enough. Passion cherishes every second of time together—in thought and in flesh.

We were sensually created—with word, hand-formed and fashioned by God himself. His breath became mankind's breath. We are created to hear, smell, feel, and taste each other. Passion takes time to tap into the sensual side of our humanity. Passion is an expression of our nature, a characteristic of our creation. A husband and wife should feel free to be as sensual as they desire. Be it loud screams or gentle moans, soft whispers or unnatural noises. Be free!!

Ahhhh, passion!

1
Erotic, Adventurous Sex

This chapter must be prefaced with the understanding that I believe all sexual behaviors must be healthy, loving, and mutually agreeable. Generally speaking, in my opinion, as long as *both* partners agree, anything goes. If it's not fun for both, it's not fun. There's always the question of what's "right" or "okay" in the sexual experience you share with your spouse. I believe that all consensual sex in marriage is sacred.

The definition of erotic has come to mean something perverted and inherently wrong. The dictionary defines erotic as "tending to arouse sexual love or desire." Erotic, arousing sexual love or desire, wow! Now that doesn't seem so perverted to me. Erotic sex, *eros,* can bring joy into a marital relationship.

It's good for married couples to experiment with preferred sexual positions and locations. In my opinion, the married sex life should be full of variety. This is the only person you will be having sex with for the rest of your married life. Going on erotic, passionate, sexual adventures will keep the relationship fresh, the fire burning, and the imagination racing! Erotica keeps the embers burning, the desires churning, the moans moaning and gives groans new groaning. Erotica drowns out the mundane and renews excitement again and again.

Erotic sex may include role playing and dress up. I've heard women say things like, "If I have to be someone else in order for him to be aroused then he can just get someone else." I heard a preacher on television once state that if a couple was role playing they were committing adultery in their hearts because they were having sex with someone else. My response: Get a grip!

Although my husband has never asked, if he wanted me to dress us like Wonder Woman I'd show him what a Super Heroine I could be!! If he wanted me to dress up like a maid I'd tickle all of his fancies with my feather duster. Really, if it turns him on then it turns me on.

Erotic sex may include different positions. I used to believe that the missionary position was the only position one could do it in and not be "dirty." I have since come to understand that God does not care if we do it upside down. I believe that most of us learned about doing it "doggy style" or standing up in the shower, or on the kitchen table from movies that dishonored the sexual act. Usually these scenes are when someone is committing adultery or doing it with a prostitute or with someone they just met. The message gets into our brains that only trifling women do these things. The message we should be getting is that a lot of our husbands *like* to do these things and we need to get on board (so to speak).

Open communication is vital to enjoying your sexual relationship. You have to be comfortable enough to say, "I don't like that" or "Will you do this?" Set your ground rules before you are all hot and bothered. In the heat of the moment it's easy to just go with the flow and then feel bad about it later.

I had the privilege of chatting candidly with an elderly woman who has been widowed for many years. She was reminiscing about the sexual adventures she and her husband enjoyed. She shared with me how they'd sneak off to the basement while the kids played up-stairs. She told me, with dancing eyes, how she and her husband slipped off to the garage in the backyard and how they spent their hunting date having "fun" on a log in the woods. She said they laughed about that all the way home. Erotic sex isn't always about the gidgets and gadgets, the positions and postures. Pure ecstasy can be found in the ability to enjoy each other wherever, whenever the moment rises.

II
Alternative Sex

Even as I prepare to type this, I am a bit nervous about how this section will be received. For those who are more conservative in their ideas this chapter will be shocking and maybe even disturbing. Don't throw the baby out with the bath water. As with all advice and opinions take what's for you and file or toss what's not.

Married couples should feel neither ashamed nor inhibited when it comes to the marriage bed. In talking about this subject with some girlfriends I was asked my notions on alternative sex options such as oral sex and anal sex. After careful consideration and researching the scriptures I am convinced that all of it is okay as long as it is okay with both spouses.

Oral sex is not prohibited by any part of our scriptures. I've been taught that if the Bible is silent on an issue the preacher ought also be. Sometimes silence is a sin.

The problem with oral sex is that it has been associated with whores. If that's your hang up I implore you to shake that off, and get counseling if you must. If you really do not enjoy performing or receiving you should not feel obligated or be forced. Not enjoying is different than feeling inhibited by oppressive teachings or being suppressed by your own mental blocks. While I believe a spouse should be *willing* to do things they do not like, occasionally, a spouse should never be *forced* or *shamed* into doing what they do not like—ever!

Anal sex is possibly the most controversial of all. One of the inhibitors for Christians is the teachings against sodomy in the Old Testament. By definition sodomy is between two persons of the same gender. Therefore, this would not be applicable to a husband and wife.

There are health risks, the obvious being the transfer of potentially harmful bacteria. Another health risk is in tearing her colon. Since the woman's health is at greatest risk this should be *her* decision and, as with all sexual adventures, mutually agreeable.

I caution you in all of your relational adventures to check them out against your marital vows to "love, honor, and cherish." Your spouse should be your friend and therefore, there should be a demonstration of love toward one another. When the line is crossed in one area of the relationship it is more likely to be crossed in other areas of your relationship.

Do not let the fear of sin keep you from enjoying the adventures of erotic sex. Remember, God doesn't see how others see; God is looking at the thoughts and the intents of our hearts *(I Samuel 16:7)*. If the heart is pure the sex will be also. Have fun, be free. Enjoy your body; enjoy your spouse's body. In the bedroom you don't have to be parents or professionals, you are just two lovers doing your "groove thang!"

Part Four
Sexuality and Playful Expression

"Pusuit and seduction are the essence of sexiality. It's part pf the sizzle."

Camille Paglia

"A merry heart doeth good like a medicine"
Proverbs 17:22

Sometimes you've just gotta have some fun! Marriage has to involve light-hearted, nonsensical fun from time to time. Life, especially married life, is very demanding. Often, life is full of serious responsibilities. I am not a professional in the emotions; however, it seems to me that light-hearted fun could do a lot to improve a person as well as a marriage.

When a couple plays together it is an indication that they really like each other, that they are friends. It's a pleasure to be open and expressive with a person you like and love! Being playful keeps the relationship light hearted and duty free. A couple who can enjoy each other's company will be able to enjoy each other's "company." In the next two chapters I'll talk about two ways to be playful—flirting and dating. Certainly these are not the only ways to be playful. Please, feel free to find your own way!

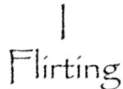

Flirting

In some movie I watched years ago a horny teenage boy said to a girl, "Hey baby, can I put my horse in your barn?" This is so hilarious to me!! It's ridiculous, but hilarious! If you have a silly personality you could really have fun creating ridiculous, hilarious sexual invitations.

My husband and I attended a community worship service one winter night. We were preparing our departure and at this point we were standing with two of our members when he told me he was riding home with someone else. "Oh," I said, "I wanted you to pump my gas tonight." Very nonchalantly he said, "I want to pump your gas tonight." I turned bright red and my eyes bugged out. I excused myself quickly. I was a little embarrassed, but it was funny as all get out! Probably no one knew what he was insinuating. More than embarrassed I was excited. I could not wait to get home! Needless to say, he pumped my gas that night!

Stephen flirts with me at the most unusual times and in the most unusual places. For example, we were sitting in a church service and he was, on the sly, rubbing my legs with his fingers. He put his arm around me and teasingly touched my neck in *that* place. He was kinda getting to me. I had to give him *the look* to make him stop. We laughed about it at home later that night.

My flirting is not so subtle, then again my personality is not subtle. Once when Stephen was complimenting me in public I said, "Well, I'll thank you for that *later*!" and winked at him with a real big wink, complete with a tongue-to-teeth click. Of course that got quite a bit of fun attention from those around us.

Flirting, whether it is subtle or all out in the open says to the other that they are being thought of sexually long before they are in the bed. Flirting entices the spouses to want something more. Flirting gives a peek into what is to come. Flirting reminds a partner of what has been. Flirting is a playful way to say, "I want you, I want to give myself to you, and I cannot wait to be with you." Flirting is very sexy.

II
Dating

Dating can be as simple or elaborate as you choose. It is so easy to make excuses as to why you cannot date—no time, no money, no energy. I feel compelled to tell you that you must get past your excuses. Every problem has a solution and where there's a will there's a way. While weekly date night is optimum, it is not realistic for most of us. Decide what is realistic for you and do that. Stephen and I have had a variety of dating experiences. We've gotten up early and went to the neighborhood McDonald's to stare at each other and chat. We sometimes walk in our neighborhood together. Sometimes we just watch television together. Occasionally, we go to a movie or out to dinner. Occasionally, we go to a park. Once we rode the city bus to the movies and then to a popular dining area and back home. The bus was part of the adventure!

The point of date time is to spend time together being friends—not parents or business partners, just friends. The rule of dating we follow is simple, "no shop talk." We can talk about dreams, share childhood stories, talk about what happened at work. We can talk about anything except parenting, bills, complaints, and plans. No mood spoilers. No diversions. It's easy to talk about the kids when there's nothing else to say. If you don't have anything to talk about create something. Use a conversation starter like, "When did you learn to ride a bike?" Or, "Tell me about the book you're reading now."

I know that many marital therapists, self-help books and such say to have a weekly date night. Honestly, I have not been able to make that work for any length of time and I don't know of my married friends who do. Stephen and I have set aside Wednesday evenings and we've set aside Saturday mornings. We've set aside evening time and we've set aside early mornings. Trying to force a night began to make the date feel like just another scheduled obligation. Right now we do not have a pattern in regards to time of day or frequency. Our lives are busy and our schedules are often chaotic. We do make it a point to have "just us" time as soon as one of us is missing the other. One of us will simply say, "I'm really missing you, I need to spend time with you." We usually spend about two days a month together just being a couple and sporadic time in between. This works for us.

Each couple must find what works for them and work it. You will always be able to find a reason, an excuse, for not doing what you need to do to preserve your marriage. Hear my caution: If you do not figure out how to work it out now you'll be crying later wondering, "What went wrong?"

Girlfriends have shared with me that date night means sex has to happen. One girlfriend shared with me that she hated dating because her husband felt like she owed him sex afterwards. I'll share some different perspectives with you.

To my sisters: First of all, let's be honest before many were married date night *did* mean sex. So, this expectation may be one you created. Secondly, for some men dating is foreplay. Not having sex at the end of the date is like *almost* going all the way. It's frustrating for him, especially if he is trying to please you. And finally, consider this notion: Perhaps you've been nagging him to do something fun. He finally caves in because you've been holding out on him. Perhaps he thinks that if he goes on a walk or to a movie (*or whatever*) that you'll want him. Then you don't want him. What's a man to think? If it's not because he didn't take you out then he'll believe it's because you just don't want him. He may feel tricked, hurt, and throw a tantrum or shut down.

To my brothers: Having fun together is like making deposits in a bank. These deposits grow interest. When you make a withdrawal there's still something there. A mystery of the spirituality of sexuality is found in that even when one is making a withdrawal they are simultaneously making another deposit. This is an awesome wonder of God.

We live in such an instantaneous society. We think that if we date tonight it should mean that we get sex tonight. One of the greatest treats about marriage is that we don't have to do it every opportunity we have—we have limitless opportunities.

It is easy for women to feel as if all you want is her body and that the date was a trick to get it. Women see dating as bonding, it's like cuddling. Consider that the reason she was able to give *it* to you when you weren't married (if that was the case) or early marriage is because you showed an interest in who she was. You complimented her, flirted with her, and wooed her.

Sometimes deposits are not available for immediate withdrawal. Sometimes a check has to be held to make sure it clears before it is credited to your account. If you have a good credit history with the bank your checks will clear more quickly, there may be no hold on it at all. Withdrawing too soon will create a negative balance. Do you get what I'm saying here? Your dating gesture is like a check—if you are in good standing your check will clear more quickly. If you have a history of ignoring your wife, criticizing her, or acting like a sex crazed teenager your check will take longer to clear. She needs to know that her value in your life is far beyond the bedroom.

As I write I am in California and Stephen is in Missouri. My nose is tingly and my eyes are watery. As I sit here telling you how my husband flirts with me, how we tease each other, how we enjoy each other's company I can see his face. Once when we were dating I caught him just staring at me. He had a sparkle in his eyes. His skin had a glow. I see him looking at me with that face even now after eight years of marriage. I see it when he's flirting. I see it when we're dating. I see it when we're chatting. And today, a thousand miles away, I can *see* his face with *that* look. The emotional impact of the memory is imprinted on my brain and in my spirit. I can *feel* him although we are more than a thousand miles apart. This is the power of flirting and dating.

The deposits Stephen has made in my spirit compel me to return to St. Louis, to him. The deposits he has made in my spirit makes me feel connected when we are miles apart. Having fun together, flirting and dating, will bring you through difficulties and life challenges will build your friendship and increase your desire for one another.

If the issue of dating for you is logistical, work it out. You'll be ever grateful you did. If the issue of dating is emotional remember to be benevolent in giving the gift of yourself. Men, remember that women need more than a penis to feel connected. Women, remember that to your husband, the issue just may not be that deep. Cut him some slack. If you cannot work through it together, please, get help.

The point of this matter is to have fun. Enjoy your time together, in and out of bed. Have a pillow fight. The more often you share fun outside the bedroom, the more likely you are to experience fun in the bedroom. Enjoy your spouse—remember the friendship you shared prior to marriage—marriage, after all, is simply being friends *with benefits!*

Part Five
Sexuality and Prohibitions

Sex is more than an act of pleasure, it's the ability to be able to feel so close to a person, so connected, so comfortable that it's almost breathtaking to the point you feel you can't take it. And at this moment you're a part of them.

Author Unknown

As I wrap this work up I feel a sense of heaviness for the women who will read this and feel even more oppressed, deficient, or unfulfilled than before. The latter two sections are written from the perspective of a woman who has a reasonable amount of emotional health to women, primarily, who have a reasonable amount of emotional health.

But I've been on the other side. I've been ashamed of my body, I've been belittled, I've been disgraced, I've been forced and ridiculed. I know what it is to not enjoy sex and to be made to feel like there was something *wrong* with me because of it.

As it is the goal of this work is to bring a sense of liberation to women, in particular, I feel compelled to explicitly discuss some of the concerns which prohibit women from enjoying a fulfilling healthy sexual relationship.

While it would be wonderful for every husband and fiancé to read this entire work, if he only reads this section I believe that your marriage will be blessed.

1
Really, It's Not You, It's Me

There are a variety of health reasons for a person's lack of libido. I think it would be natural for a spouse to feel dissed if their mate (should I say *when* their mate) has a low-to-no sex drive. It might be hard for a spouse to understand that it has nothing to do with them at all.

Stress, perhaps, is one of the chief causes of reduced sexual pleasure. When a partner is stressed it will affect how he or she is able to relate to the other. For some, when they are stressed they simply shut down, emotionally and physically. Some are more aggressive and need to physically release the pent-up pressure. Generally speaking, not absolute, a person's sexual response to stress will mirror their emotional response. For example, a person who curls up in a ball under the pressure of stress is unlikely to be wild and aggressive in the bed.

Medications, including antidepressants, antihistamines, birth control pills, and blood pressure pills are known to kill the sex drive.

Fatigue, hormone changes, menopause, and a number of diseases such as diabetes, heart problems, cancer, and arthritis can all cause a person to have a reduced desire for sexual desire.

Exercise will do much for sexual dysfunction. Thirty minutes of cardio can do the same as some medications. Of course, consult your physician and make a plan that works for you.

Whatever the reason for your partner's low sex drive you must remember that your sexual connection has created a spiritual tie. The tie in your spirit ought to inspire within each one compassion and empathy.

It is understandable that one spouse may be frustrated and irritated when the sex drive of the other dissipates. Exercise is good for frustration, too. There are many ways to be intimate without engaging in sexual intercourse. Remember your vow "To love, honor, and cherish, in *sickness* and in health?" Love is patient and kind, does not seek its own...love your spouse.

II
Body Image

The view we have of our bodies will greatly impact our ability to share ourselves with our spouse. I do not know how men's perceptions of themselves affect their sex drive, but I do know that women will shut down when they are made to feel unattractive. I am overweight by at least thirty pounds. My husband never criticizes my weight although he does, on occasion, speak to me about it—usually when I bring it up. He says to me that he loves me and wants to live a long, healthy, active life with me. He is concerned about my health and well-being more so than my appearance. Now, I know that appearance is important to him; we've spoken candidly about it. Men are more visually-stimulated than women, generally speaking. He is wise enough to know that criticizing is the quickest way to shut a person down and he loves me too much to crush me.

I often complain about aspects of my body that I cannot change without surgery—my breasts are too small and my lips are too thin. These are my two biggest self- complaints. Stephen tells me that I am just the way God made me and he loves what God made.

Stephen reassures me in regards to my body image. Because I can trust him with my heart I can trust him with my body. I know that he will not hurt me, use me, or dog me. I know that when he has an erection, it is me he wants. Although I know that temptation is ever present, I am confident because of his love for me that he will always satisfy his appetite at home.

As women, when we feel bad about how we look it prohibits

us from sharing ourselves freely. If we feel ashamed we'll hide—in the dark, under baggy clothes, under the covers, under the weather, under being too tired, under being too busy. You get the picture. The more confident a woman feels about who she is the more confident she'll feel about what she can and *wants* to do.

Women we cannot wait on our husbands to *make* us feel good. This is something that we have to work out inside ourselves. Sometimes we have to work it out with a counselor or spiritual advisor; sometimes with a friend; sometimes through prayer. Sometimes we have to work it out through doing what it takes to improve what we are unhappy with about ourselves. Knowing that I am overweight and not actively trying to do anything about it I find it a blessing that my husband still wants to be with me. So I am certainly not going to give the devil place in my relationship.

Now, don't get me wrong here. I don't believe my husband would be unfaithful even if I weighed a ton. I believe he loves God more than he loves me. I believe that he views his commitment to our marriage as his commitment to God and therefore would not violate the marital covenant. As much as I am sure he loves the Lord and loves me I am not naïve enough to think for a second that he would not be tempted, interested, or distracted by an hour glass figure.

Sisters, do the best you can with what you've got. Your husband loves *you*. All of you. Too big, too small. He loves *you*. It's *you* he wants to smell. It's *you* he wants to feel. It *you* he wants to taste. It's *you* he wants to hear calling out his name. Deal with your issues. Don't let your self image prohibit you from sharing yourself with your husband. Give him *you.*

Brothers, affirm your wife's beauty. If it's not her booty talk about her eyes, skin, hair, fingernails, spirit. Let her know how much she means to you, how valued she is, how you'd be lost without her. Let her know that your life is better because she's in it. Let her know that your commitment is to *her.*

Here's some advice for you: don't tell her that her weight (or nose, or boobs, or whatever her issue is) doesn't matter to you. She'll likely never believe you and you'll discredit *everything* you say. Whatever you do, don't tell her that her weight (or whatever) *does* matter. This is fatal. If you aren't sure what to say, just tell her over and over and over and over through words and actions how much you love her.

Women, remember that you are created in God's image and likeness. What you may see as a flaw, God designed to make you unique—like a collector's item. God has made you the way He designed. What you speak against yourself you speak against Him.

Part of the spirituality of our sexuality is in recognizing, accepting, and affirming all of who we are and being willing to share ourselves with our lovers.

|||
Taboos

Women are taught that so many things about sex is wrong, many of the topics discussed in this work fall into the category of "wrong." If you take nothing else from this work I pray you take the message that all consensual marital sex is pure and holy unto God. I pray that you will allow yourself the freedom of exploring and growing in your sexual self.

For centuries people believed that the world was flat because that is what they had been taught. Columbus had the courage to explore, to learn for himself. This is what we have to do, too. Have the courage to explore the taboos of the sexual relationship. It is liberating to know that I don't do things I don't do because of my *choice* as opposed to someone's imposed rules. It's liberating to know that I can *enjoy* what I do without feeling like my physical pleasure is doing a spiritual harm.

Husbands, I urge you to be compassionate, allow your wife the time and space to explore sexually. If she has believed, for example, that oral sex or masturbation was wrong for many years this view and the emotional impact of the view is unlikely to change overnight. It is a process. Please be patient and loving toward your wife. She will let you know when she is ready to explore.

Prayer works miracles!! God cares about your sexual pleasure. Ask God to heal your wife. Ask God to tame your appetite. Ask God for His grace over your relationship.

Because our sexuality is intertwined with our spirituality, being healed in our spirit will free us to be healed in our sexual perceptions.

IV
Traumas

It is only on occasion that I meet a woman who was not sexually abused as a child, or raped by a relative, stranger, date, or spouse. I do not know if there are more instances of sexual traumas in this day or if they are just being reported more often. More and more we are hearing also about men who have been sexually traumatized.

Being traumatized in childhood can adversely affect a person's ability to relax and enjoy the sexual pleasures of marriage. Being inhibited can be confusing for a spouse if they were sexually active prior to marriage. I will not attempt to deal with the psychology of this topic. I will urge both husband and wife to seek professional therapy. Hurts are inhibitors to pleasure. Keeping the traumas trapped inside oneself takes up the space pleasure would otherwise occupy. Sometimes we've just got to clean our closets out of the old stuff to make room for some new stuff.

I also urge spouses to be patient, compassionate, and loving toward their spouse. I *thought* I was healed of the affects of my sexual traumas. After Stephen and I were married I discovered how much junk was still in my "closet." It is because he was so kind and compassionate that I knew certain problems we had were *mine*. I knew that I had to work on my issues.

One issue I had was Stephen leaving the house. Early in our marriage I obsessively asked Stephen, "Where are you going?" Actually, I asked this when he simply got up to walk to another room. I am sure this issue was born from my previous marriage and being traumatized knowing that he was leaving home to be with someone else.

Instead of Stephen reacting harshly he responded with compassion. One day he started answering, "I'm going to give you a kiss and then I'm going…(to get some water *or whatever*)." Over time, because of his compassion, the unconscious fear that he was leaving me dissipated.

I am not at liberty to speak about my husband's issues early in our marriage. I can tell you, however, that I responded with compassion, stroking his ego and affirming his *greatness* (wink, wink).

Showing compassion is what a friend does for a friend. As we grow in friendship with our spouses, I believe that we will be able to journey through healing *together*, refining one another, holding one another up during difficulties. It is because of the friendship my husband and I share that I am able to pen the words on the pages of this work.

Final Thoughts

Allow yourself the freedom to physically love without all of the hook-ups of someone else's expectations and the stress of traumas caused by someone else. Whatever your experiences were in the past, they are now in the past. When we hold onto our traumas we are allowing the offender to offend us over and over again. Whatever you were taught when you were younger must be put into context and evaluated for present day relevancy. As best you are able, live your life in the present, experience the joy of your now. Let your only expectation be to give and receive pleasure.

Give yourself permission to enjoy your sexuality. Give yourself permission to enjoy a sensual, sexual relationship with your spouse. Give yourself permission to heal and grow. Give yourself permission to learn, experiment, and most of all—have fun.

The gift of sexuality can be a source of excitement, amusement, entertainment, comfort, and peace. Receive God's gift of sexual desires and longings. Enjoy God's gift of pleasure and passion. Enjoy God's gift of love and adventure.

Enjoying great sex will make your spirit and your body shout

Holy Moly!

Resources

Below is a list of articles I read along the way as I wrote. You can easily conduct your own research on topics by googling specific words or phrases. This can be exhausting! I've only included one or two for each topic. There are so many perspectives! Mostly I looked to see if my thoughts were just mine or if anyone in the cyber world held a similar view. I also looked for differing perspectives to challenge my own views. In some cases I admittedly had to say, "well, I can appreciate that view" even if I didn't necessarily agree.

Enjoy your researching and reviewing!!

First Impressions

http://www.isnare.com/?aid=221540&ca=Career
http://entrepreneurs.about.com/cs/marketing/a/uc051603a.htm

Offenses

http://www.femalepatient.com/html/arc/sel/march02/article04.asp
http://www.albionmonitor.com/free2/abusesickness.html
http://www.humanitarianreform.org/humanitarianreform

Boys and Sexual Abuse

http://member.preventchildabuse.org/site/DocServer/sexual_abuse_of_
boys.pdf?docID=127
http://www.sasian.org/papers/boysngirls.htm

Date Rape

http://www.aaets.org/article13.htm
http://www.ulv.edu/ctimes/bestoct/hall/daterape.htm
http://www.aic.gov.au/publications/tandi/ti157.pdf

Abuse Attraction

http://net-burst.net/hope/survivor.htm
http://www.youcanhaveitall.com/articles/relationships-peggy.html

Senior Sexual Abuse

http://seniorjournal.com/NEWS/Eldercare/4-11-09SexualAbuse.htm

Mental Sex

http://www.cybercollege.com/sexrsh-2.htm

Remorseful/Make Up Sex

http://shine.yahoo.com/channel/sex/7-reasons-for-make-up-sex-361215/?posted=1

Sex as a Bargaining Tool

http://www.ivillage.co.uk/relationships/couple/right/articles/0,,144_626619-3,00.html

Physiological Benefits of Sex

http://www.msnbc.msn.com/id/28146086/
http://news.bbc.co.uk/1/hi/health/1194887.stm

Effects of Laughter

http://women.webmd.com/guide/give-your-body-boost-with-laughter#
http://health.blogs.foxnews.com/2009/01/12/sepert-qa-sex-is-no-laughing-matter-%E2%80%93-or-is-it/

Printed in the United States
145657LV00002B/3/P